Kaocentric Marketing and the Sorcery of Sales

Nathan Dube

Published by Nathan Dube, 2024.

While every precaution has been taken in the preparation of this book, the publisher assumes no responsibility for errors or omissions, or for damages resulting from the use of the information contained herein.

KAOCENTRIC MARKETING AND THE SORCERY OF SALES

First edition. January 15, 2024.

ISBN: 979-8224462025

Written by Nathan Dube.

Table of Contents

Kaocentric Marketing

By Nathan Dube

A Note About Magic(k)

For those of you who are new to the concept of magic outside of its use in fictional narratives and other forms of storytelling, I would like to present a word about the subject.

Basically, magic is using your will power to cause changes in reality. While magic can be used for many things, I primarily use it to better my life. Done properly, so can you.

Now, first things first. Magic is NOT evil. Magic is a TOOL. For example, magic is, in some ways, similar to a hammer. You can use a hammer to build a house for a homeless person. You can also use a hammer to harm or kill someone. The hammer itself is not evil.

What you do with the hammer affects your moral ecosystem by way of what you choose to use the hammer for. And so, it is the same with magic. For the more conservative readers of this book, think of it like this. Magic is not unlike a gun.

For those of you who are diametrically opposed to alternative spiritualities or, what some may call "woo-woo", and it's related topics, I would ask you to consider reading this book from the perspective of the psychological model of magic.

I would make the same recommendation for the ultra-religious person who may believe their clergy's propaganda against the practice of the magical arts.

As for how magic works, well, that can be defined through five models or perspectives. These models are as follows:

The Psychological Model: The psychological model of magic reduces the art to a purely psychological practice in which any changes the magician makes to the outside world is accomplished only as a byproduct from the internal changes that happen to the practitioner when performing magical acts.

These acts are including but not limited to, spell work, ritual, enchantment, evocation, invocation, meditation, and so on. It is from this perspective that one who is averse to religion or spirituality may be able to find value from the performance of magical endeavors as an experiment to improve one's life.

The Energetic Model: This model of magic postulates that all magic is done through the use of manipulating energy sources and moving said energy through magical practices that direct and enhance the energy in a effort to cause change in physical reality. An excellent example of the energy in question would be that of which is commonly used in the healing practice of reiki.

The Spirit Model: In the spirit model of magic, all magical acts are accomplished exclusively by spirits of which the magician can "work" with through acts of evocation, invocation, and enchantments of various kinds. For the sake of an example, you could argue that a Catholic mass is essentially a kind of spirit-based ritual magic.

The Information Model: The information model of magic suggests the acquisition of as much information as possible prior to a magical operation, which is then used to direct the actions and/or energy of a magical operation, is, in fact, the key to the success of said operation.

The Meta-Model: Finally, we have the meta-model of magic. This model suggests that magic is an intricate art and science that works via a combination of two or more of the above models to produce results.

Personally, I work within the meta-model as it seems to be the best model for a practicing chaos magician such as myself. The meta-model is highly useful when paradigm-shifting through belief systems to produce magic.

I refer to the combination of chaos magic and the sales and marketing techniques in this book as "Kaocentric," meaning that the magical applications herein lean heavily on the side of chaos magical approaches in the context of a meta-model perspective.

If you are new to the practice of magic, I would suggest approaching this book through the psychological model before attempting to understand it from other perspectives.

Preface:

Chaos magic is an approach to the psychological and/or metaphysical work of causing a change in reality through the manipulation or focusing of will power into the act of ritual or spell work. The intention behind this work being to bring forth the manifestation of one's desires.

If you are the type of person who thinks all spirituality is complete and utter bullshit, this book may not be for you. However, chaos magic can be done by both the nun and the atheist alike.

How so?

One of the central tenets of chaos magic is the ability to entirely, albeit temporarily, adopt a belief system in order to use that belief system's worldview to produce magical results that would otherwise be impossible without the context of said belief system.

For example, if you would like to conjure an archangel or a demon in order to use their skills to fulfill the manifestation of a desire, you would likely get better results by temporarily adopting the Christian worldview for the duration of the spell, ritual or other magical work that you are producing.

Once the work has been completed, you can simply let go of the beliefs if they no longer serve you or your future intentions.

This can be particularly hard for those who are incredibly devout to a specific religion or lack thereof (atheism), but for those who are willing to put in the effort for such an endeavor, there are great rewards in the ability to shift and explore one's mind in these ways.

There is an absolute freedom that comes with the ability once a person has been able to do this with ease, which provides the magician with, if nothing else, a profound kind of psychological liberty.

The practical examples in this book which are designed to inspire your own magical experiments are a combination of chaos magic, other types of magic, and both traditional and modern marketing and sales techniques.

Done with a sense of gusto and determination, those who are willing to put time and effort into reproducing or building similar magical operations to those mentioned within these pages, will find that reality will begin to act strangely in response to said magical work.

Essentially, you will find that the universe has taken notice of you and that it has decided to work with you in an effort to help in the manifestation of your desired outcomes.

As with any other art or science, further study and practice are recommended. **It should be duly noted that you will only gain from these practices what you put into them.**

While this work does not require a belief, or dare I say, "faith," in the context of the idea of magic being real, temporarily adopting this belief as an initiatory step in the act of paradigm-shifting belief systems will increase the probability of earlier success with the tools presented in this book.

Foreword:

This book is not an introduction to magic. Nor is it such a tome for sales and marketing. This book is a practical manual for those who are interested in where the crossroads of magic, marketing, and sales meet. It is a workbook for those who are interested in implementing a combination of all three in order to manifest their ultimate dreams and goals.

This book is written for people who care about magic, marketing, and sales. If you are alive and breathing today, in theory, that should be you. Your personal brand is your key to success. As the owner of your personal brand, you must be able to market and sell yourself as well as the brand and products produced by the company you choose to work for whether it be your own business or another's.

Those with a background in sales and marketing will likely get the most out of this book; however, the examples in this guide, if put into action, will be useful to all who are willing to experiment with the ideas within.

Consider these pages gasoline and the reading of them the spark of a flame called creativity. Understand, this is a book for those who want to make waves and for those who understand that the skills garnered from practicing magic, marketing, and sales techniques, mainly when combined together, may produce results that border on the miraculous.

Regardless of what you call this power: faith, will, energy, god, spirit, electricity, knowledge, wisdom, thought...

This book offers those who understand that change is made via the application of desire to the lever of willpower, the perspective management capabilities to re-enchant their life, career, and the world at large.

As for me, I used magic to manifest the job, house, and life of my dreams, and I will continue to expand upon those achievements, all the while presenting my work and experiments in objects such as this book.

The magical technology mentioned herein is meant to inspire your own magical actions and experimentations so that you may find yourself in a similar position.

Quite simply, this book is a working example of how to use magic in tandem with marketing and sales techniques to live with and embody a perpetual state of joy and contentment.

Introduction: A Story of Success

Below you will find a success report that details how I used magic to manifest the life I have always wanted. This was originally written and shared with members of Jason Miller's Strategic Sorcery[1] course (a magical education course that I HIGHLY recommend).

Ok, so, here is the full success report on manifesting my dream house, life, and career. This is a long story, as it is a multi-year process that spanned

---

1.　　http://www.strategicsorcery.net/courses/strategic-sorcery-course/

a few colossal life transformations. However, I wanted to paint the full picture of the value of the strategic sorcery course...

How I manifested my dream house with the use of magic

For many years, my wife and I have always dreamed of owning a waterfront property, either on a lake or by the sea. For a long time, it seemed out of reach. But as I started practicing magic and with my wife doing some metaphysical work as well, we slowly built our careers to a point where the goal was not only reachable but primed for manifestation. This goal was ultimately achieved via a concerted effort in both magical and mundane work towards the goal.

In this essay, I will attempt to give as concise an explanation as possible about the magic that was performed and the results that were garnered through these mystical arts.

When I first began studying magic, I was primarily reading into it to "know my enemy." I had been raised Christian and taught to fear any religion or mystical practices that were not from Christian teachings, particularly occultism.

Visions of an eternity in hellfire and being tortured by demons for being a sinner was the standard fare for messages presented at most of the youth gatherings in the various churches and denominations I was paraded through as a child.

To say that these teachings left an immense smoking crater of trauma that would haunt me spiritually, physically, mentally, and emotionally would be the understatement of the decade.

In fact, the single most outstanding magical achievement for me personally was using my magical practice as a way to escape and heal from the wounds caused by Christianity. Leaving that religion was the most profound and healing action I have ever taken upon myself, but that story is for another day.

Now, I had been studying world religions, witchcraft, mysticism, and other spiritual topics since I was about 14. I began researching magic between the ages of 18 and 19. At the age of 21, I found myself working in what felt like a dead-end job. I was working as a retail clerk assistant in a print shop for a supervisor who hated me and treated me like a complete moron and second class citizen.

To rub salt in the wound, I was never hired to work in retail. I was hired to be a graphic designer for a local B2B printer and copier dealer; however, shortly after getting hired, I was told I would be working retail instead. I told my boss, that was not in my job description. We both just laughed and laughed and laughed...

During my time at the print shop, I would also be moved around the company to do various odd jobs in addition to my retail duties. Everything from landscaping to refilling inkjets in the production warehouse (a rather filthy job which I was almost able to get onto the Discovery Channel's "Dirty Jobs" show). It became rare that I was actually able to do any of the things I had originally been hired to do.

While working at the print shop, there were times where I could work at a computer. Alone in the back room, I would study magic while working on customer projects that involved printing thousands of simple documents, a process of which, often took hours for the printer to complete.

At 21, I found myself suffering from extreme tunnel vision. I found myself thinking that I would absolutely hate eight hours of my life every day for the rest of my life until retirement. And then, I came across hermeticism.

The hermetic philosophy was the first occult information that I had come across that made me truly question the validity of Christianity's claim to have a corner on the market of truth. There are many things that happened between then and now, but for the sake of brevity; I will focus on the following events.

I began seriously practicing magic in 2010. Then, in 2012, I came across Gordon White's famous blog post on sigil magic[2]. *This lead me to read a* lot of his content and helped me to discover other great practicing magicians *such as Jason Miller, Rufus Opus, Jake Stratton-Kent, Ian Cat Vincent,*

---

2.   https://runesoup.com/2012/03/ultimate-sigil-magic-guide/

Taylor Ellwood, Ramsey Dukes, Peter Carol, Phil Hein, Tommie Kelly, Julio Ody, and a whole host of other prominent practitioners of magic.

After researching tons of magical blogs and books over the next three years, I eventually decided I wanted to enter Jason Miller's Strategic Sorcery course, which I completed over the course of a year. While Jason's course is not the only magical course I have taken, the strategic sorcery course is one of the best classes on practical magic I have ever come across.

The course is extremely "Kaocentric" and borrows from various magical traditions. The final product is a collection of information on how to do potent spell work, divination, offerings, evocation, invocation, protection and reversal magic, wealth magic, working with deities, and a host of other fundamentals that are key to starting a proper and productive magical practice.

After I had decided I wanted to take the course, I realized that I really could not afford the $150 price tag at the time. So, I decided to do some magic to get the course paid for by my company as I felt I could spin the value of the course as useful towards social media marketing and sales (which proved to be absolutely TRUE).

*At this point in time, I had moved up in the company to a position as the social media manager, and at the same time, I became a member of the sales team (after three years of continually being placed onto odd jobs, I had finally secured a position that I was not only proud of, but actually **really loved**).*

As getting a better position in the business was partly accomplished via the help of Gordon White's sigil shoaling technique, I decided to use it to try to get the company to pay for the strategic sorcery course. I charged a shoal of sigils each with variations of the intent being to get my boss to approve my course as a company expense.

When trying to figure out how I would sell him on the idea, I decided to take a considerable risk. As he knew that I was interested in the magical arts, metaphysics, and spirituality, I could tell he was curious about my ideas.

He himself seemed open to things such as Buddhism and philosophy. I asked for the opportunity to do a short fifteen-minute presentation for him in our board room. For that time, I spoke about chaos magic with an emphasis on the art of sigilization and how it can be applied to marketing and sales.

To my great surprise, he accepted my presentation a couple of days later. I relayed all the information above, showing him how to create and charge sigils while drawing comparisons to the creation and deployment of corporate logos.

I shared my ideas on color theory and advertising and how there is an obvious crossover between the psychology of magic and the art of advertising.

At the end of my presentation, I expressed great interest in bettering my understanding of how magical technologies could be used in successful marketing and sales campaigns and made my case for the strategic sorcery course.

When I finished, he thought silently for about a minute, reviewing the presentation in his head while looking at the examples, notes, and diagrams I had drawn on the whiteboard during my presentation.

I can see the value in this, he said with a smile. He continued speaking, saying: as a business expense, one hundred and fifty dollars is not much at all; just sign up for the course today, and I will have our finance department cut you a check for the cost.

I thanked him and expressed my genuine gratitude for the opportunity to take the course and be able to leverage the wisdom within and apply it to my efforts in the arts of marketing and sales.

Ok BOOM... Magic. Result. Win. *< This is legit how it can work when you give a fuck, put in the effort, and invest power into the process. "Power" can mean faith, belief, energy, etc. Hell, you could use "the force" or some other fictional idea if it gives you the chutzpah to take names and kick ass.*

Once I had completed the lessons in strategic sorcery, I applied several things that I learned in the course to helping me make more money and be more successful at work. I threw spells and enchantments at sales, social media, business communications, and meetings and was able to quickly and steadily grow a successful run as a profitable salesman in the copier and printer industry.

Some of the work that I did to achieve these things at the time includes but is not limited to

- *Daily meditation.*
- *The pillar exercise.*
- *The annual Jupiter Rite (on both the days of the group working and also continually as I saw fit).*
- *Embedding the virality glyph into emails and social campaigns.*
- *Command and control oils.*
- *Sweetening spells.*
- *Hotfoot powder.*
- *Various other magical operations and technology.*

Per the instructions in the course, I began forming relationships with various spirits from a "kaocentric, meta-model perspective" of which I was implementing at the time. This is to say, that sometimes I would be approaching entities from either the spirit, energetic, psychological, or information models of magic or some combination of two or more of these perspectives.

Some of the spirits I have worked with include:

Queen Ninisinna
Papa Legba
Santa Muerte
Bune
Jupiter
Venus
Mercury
Zaphkiel
Zadkiel
Rafael

Buer
Saint Joseph
Saint Anne
Our Lady of Lourdes
Fatima

I worked with each of these personas in making offerings of light, smoke, food, drinks, prayer, devotion, and through the practices of evocation and invocation.

For example, at one point, I had hit a brick wall with a large copier sale. What should have been an easy "open and shut" case of sales success with a long-time customer, ended up being a complicated mess due to miscommunications, pricing, functionality of the device, and financing issues.

It got very frustrating for both the client and I. Eventually, I started to feel as if I was going to lose the deal. Having exhausted the mundane approaches to the problem, I decided to utilize Jason's evocation of the goetic spirit known as BUNE.

Following the instructions for the operation (which is really more of a petition, rather than an evocation), I requested Bune's assistance in moving the deal forward and removing any further pushback or obstacles. I did the petition per Jason's instructions on a riverbed in a secret spot that I have gone to over the years to meditate, pray, fish, or do magical work.

When I came out of the woods near the parking lot where my car was parked, I got a phone call. It was my client. He told me that everything had been worked out and that he was calling to purchase the machine. This was a $16,000 machine sale with about $10,000 in residual income from consumable items for the equipment. I was STOKED.

There were various experiences like this over the next five years, in the majority of which, I continued to meet or exceed my quota and closed quite a few large contract customers.

However, in late 2017, I was not selling well at all; it had been a slow six months. If you have ever worked in sales, you know this is an ominous portent. I was called into the office around noon. This is it, I thought, I am done.

My boss brought me into the conference room and sat me down. He asked how I was doing, and we made some small talk for a bit. And then, it happened. He looked at me and told me that the Executive Marketing Manager was retiring, and he wanted to offer me a promotion to the position.

I was shocked, super happy, and obviously said yes. This was a curveball coming out of left field that was dripping in synchronicities attached to sigil shoals, enchantments, spell work, and pure will power.

I accepted the position and immediately started making a game plan on how to combine digital marketing processes and magical work to help me achieve my goals as the new Executive Marketing Manager.

Through the use of a servitor, I procured almost $30,000 from a corporate partner for my business, which we were able use on marketing initiatives. Several of these projects were then used to embody the servitor in the persona of a fictional character that would serve as a kind of mascot for the company.

The servitor would prove useful in helping me to develop two film projects and a video game (that was a bucket list item right there) in which the servitor was given viral attention through social media.

It was all very heady, and a lot of success and creative juice was flowing around. So, it was yet another shock when, eight months later, I was laid off with about a dozen other employees.

My boss explained to me that neither I nor the others were being laid off due to problems associated with our work ethic. Instead, the fact was that the company had purchased a competitor, and while gaining a considerable swath of market share, the company was losing money quickly...

I was apologized to and was given a generous severance package (the number on the check being rather close to a sigil design I had recently made). I left the building and met a buddy at a bar. He bought me drinks, and I pondered the strange state I now found myself in.

Between my wife's job, the unemployment checks, and the severance, we were able to make ends meet for the almost eight months I ended up being out of work.

I had hoped this time would feel like a vacation, but the days were wrought with some of the worst anxiety attacks I had ever had in my life. The sudden and unexpected upheaval slammed me way harder than I had thought, and confusion and disdain took over for a while.

Eventually though, I refocused. I started doing the proper mundane and magical work to either start a successful business or attract the ideal career for myself. During this time, I turned down five job offers as I felt that I really needed to find the right fit. However, this brought me dangerously close to the end of my unemployment checks.

After applying for about 150 jobs, I was brought in for an interview for two positions I really wanted. Both were 100% remote work with good money and an excellent benefits package. I accepted the first job while still doing the interview process for the second job. It was the latter I really wanted, and I put a lot of magical and mundane effort into solidifying the position.

I did a sweetening spell, a sigil shoal, petitioned spirits, wore success and luck oils, and brought 150% to the interview. I landed the job.

I let the other company know I had received a better offer, and I took the position with the company that I truly wanted to work for.

It proved to be a dream job, the best career I had ever had with the most amazing co-workers in the world. I now get to do almost everything I love most. Writing, podcasting, blogging, videography, animation, music, graphic design, voice acting, and other highly creative projects.

I now make over $10,000 a year more than my last company, and I have consistent opportunities to move upward. In the first year alone, I got a raise, a $3,000 laptop, and a technology stipend. All of that on top of a top-shelf benefits package and quality sick, vacation, and bereavement time.

I have now been at this company for almost two years and still absolutely love my job, co-workers, and company. With the better pay from my job in addition to my wife's continual raises at her company of over 20 years, we soon realized that we could afford way more than we had thought in regard to a new house.

My wife crunched the numbers, and we made a plan to renovate our home. Based on the market information we collected, we figured that we could make a $20,000 profit. This would give us the down payment needed to buy our dream house, which for us, was a lakefront property that we have named "the shire" as it legit feels like a "hobbit house" to us.

So, we once again began working in both mundane and magical ways. While the house was being renovated, I began the magical preparations by burying a statue of saint joseph and reciting the proper prayers for that spell (used to sell your house). Now, this was all happening during the black swan event we have all come to know as COVID. This really made it a crazy process and genuine test of wisdom and strength.

The timing seemed absurd, but all the portents said, it was time! From the moment we listed our house on the market to the day we moved into the new lake house where I am now typing this document, I launched countless shoals, did prayers and offerings to various spirits, and did a whole slew of spells and enchantments.

This entire process was heavily inspired by the strategic sorcery course and was augmented by the work and insights of the other magicians mentioned in this article.

As for the final result, we sold our house in 48 hours to a bidder who offered full price with no haggling. We made an offer on our dream house about three months later, and we got the house!

The day we moved into the house; a hurricane was moving through town. Despite this setback and almost the whole town where we now live losing power, we got everything into the new place with no damage to our vehicles or new property.

In the end, we made a $46,000 profit from the sale of our house, more than double what we had originally calculated as likely.

So now, with our little piece of paradise, the work goes on, and we will strive to continue manifesting our goals and using magic to augment the mundane so that we can truly live the life we love.

Now, you may think, "eh, this is all just psychology or even dumb luck." Honestly, I do not care if you believe in magic or not, BUT, if you have read this far and feel a connection and are willing read on, I will say this...

If you implement the magical technologies I discuss in this book in your own life, consistently, all the while investing belief and energy into the work, you will create changes in your life that will significantly enhance the probabilities of reaching your goals and even your wildest dreams.

The remainder of this book is a deeper dive into some of the more potent and effective spells, enchantments, and magical operations that I utilized in the process of manifesting my career, dream house, and international acclaim as a guerilla marketing professional.

I will, in the following text, re-examine and reiterate the success story mentioned above while offering greater details on how I accomplished my goals. I invite you to explore my work and take from it what you find useful as you work to manifest your own dreams.

Chapter One: Reworking the Cornerstones of Chaos

There are many tools within the practice of chaos magic and marketing alike. Some of them useful, others nonsensical oddities perhaps designed to throw off fools or to keep them busy entertaining themselves. Moreover, while not all practices of chaos magic or marketing are considered viable means of accomplishing the aim of sorcery, indeed, the two cornerstones of chaos magic most certainly are.

Sigils

First and foremost, we have the process of sigilization. First introduced to the world in the form of cave drawings by early human beings and evolving over thousands of years through people such as Heinrich Cornelius Agrippa and the godfather of chaos magic himself Austin Osman Spare.

Sigilization is perhaps the most well-known technique of chaos magic in today's world. This particular art owes a significant debt to Gordon White, proprietor, author, and podcast host at runesoup.com[1].

Negating a lengthy description of the process aside, it is simplified in the following instruction.

A sigil starts as a sentence expressing a desire, for example: "I own a house by the lake." The vowels and repeating letters are subsequently removed (some people do not remove the repeating letters). The remaining letters are then combined to form a shape, glyph, or symbol.

The symbol is then "charged" via gnosis (an altered state of consciousness), which can be achieved through heavy breathing, intense exercise, meditation, yoga, the use of psychoactive drugs (such as caffeine, alcohol, or marijuana), or some other activity until the glyph is fully enhanced and imbued with psychic energy.

---

1.   https://runesoup.com/2012/03/ultimate-sigil-magic-guide/

The meaning of the glyph must then be forgotten, less the lust of result kills the seed that is the symbol being planted into the subconscious mind. Eventually, that which you initially expressed through the desire of the original sentence becomes an actual event that manifests in your life.

Forgetting the meaning of the symbol being a rather complicated challenge can be negated by the charging of multiple sigils one after another, until you have confused the meaning of which sigil pertains to which desire.

If done correctly, the symbol implants itself into the subconscious mind and grows into the physical manifestation of the desire of which the symbol represents. In this case, a house by the lake. Of course, like any skill, this takes practice, and starting with a small, more achievable goal is advised.

This technique, properly done, increases the probability of your desire manifesting. However, even if you cut the odds of winning the lottery in half, you are still essentially no closer than you were before. Aim for multiple small goals, rather than one or two ridiculously huge ones...

The second cornerstone, of course, is the idea of belief as a tool. It goes to suggest that if the magus is capable of temporarily but entirely investing belief into something such as a religion, system of spirituality, or model of magic, said belief will allow the magus to achieve things in a way that may not be possible without said investment.

And so, through the act of using belief as a tool to temporarily become a Christian, a Buddhist, a fictional character, reincarnated spirit, or any such thing that you can successfully believe yourself to be... One is able to extract useful information and technology from the experience that the temporary belief produces. These experiences can be leveraged to create change or manifest enchantments, of which one could not accomplish otherwise.

It is this, the second cornerstone of chaos magic, that I wish to expand upon in a way that differs from most of the practitioners of chaos magic and the standard way of using this technology.

The Stock Market of Belief

I have dubbed my personal approach to the practice of belief as a tool, "the stock market of belief". Unlike the traditional approach of temporarily fully investing belief into a religion, philosophy, or other systems of thought, I suggest metaphorically cutting your belief into smaller amounts. Thus, one is able to invest belief into multiple different religions, convictions, ideas, etc. without having to invest in only one fully.

The idea behind this modification of approach is based upon the idea that belief can, in fact, be invested into different things. It can be invested into several different options in the same way that money can be invested into different stocks. If the investment pays off as hoped for, more belief can be invested. If, however, you do not get the return on investment you expected, removing said investments and reinvesting elsewhere is recommended.

This process can be repeated indefinitely, *Ad infinitum*. In this way, the magician can reap the benefits of multiple concepts or belief systems simultaneously without having to fully invest in only one. This results in the faster and more efficient acquiring of useful tools and processes from each investment. In a sense, it is magical multitasking for the mage on the move.

As you continue this process, you shall find hidden gems of wisdom and practical magic which can be added to your personal practice. S/he who is willing to use this process continually, may find an ongoing and noticeable bump in synchronicities within their day to day life.

This book's foundation shall rest upon these two cornerstones mentioned above. It is my intention to leverage these tools and mechanisms as gleaned from years of study and practice as a launchpad into my personal approach to the practice of chaos magic. As such, I would recommend that you consider doing the same.

Pushing Coins Off A Ledge.

If you have ever been to a video arcade (dear lord, I am dating myself), you may have come across a "game" or rather a machine called a "coin pusher." Basically, it is a large metal box with a window in the front of the machine. Inside the box, you can see a ledge. People will insert coins, and the coin rolls down to a platform just prior to the ledge.

As time goes on, an extensive collection of coins builds up and slowly pushes the coins to the edge of the ledge. Eventually, the entire ledge will be covered in coins, half over the edge, and half still on the platform. The lucky winner who drops the right coin will push the mass of coins and drop a large amount of them into the base of the machine. The winner then collects the coins, or in most cases, the value of the coins in tickets, which can be traded in for prizes at the desk of the arcade.

To me, this machine defines the process of casting spells and enchantments. Finding a balance between timing and the condensation of coins, will result in the most successful coin flips (or spells). If you are the first one to drop a coin in a coin pusher, you know that you will not win. But find the right machine tucked into the corner of a long-forgotten arcade or pizza parlor, and you might just be in the right place at the right time.

And so it is with magic. The desires you wish to manifest with sigilization, candle spells (or any type of magic for that matter) are best made manifest by dropping the coin at the right time in the right machines. Nevertheless, how do you find those metaphorical coin pushers of life that will reward you with the best return on investment when it comes to the charging of sigils and casting of spells?

Divination is a most useful tool when considering the above question. Tarot, playing cards, dice, or even flipping a coin may yield some direction in this endeavor. For me, however, it comes down to looking for the smallest goals, with the highest possibility of going to your favor.

In this respect, sigilizing or spelling your way to winning the lottery is but a fool's errand. As such, casting a single enchantment in an attempt to acquire the house on the lake would likewise be foolish.

To work magic effectively is not hard. To work it with intelligence and patience is another game altogether. When first sitting down and contemplating the life you wish to attract or manifest into being, it is a good idea to write down the big picture... Or paint it... Or record the audio of your voice explaining the vision... Just get it out of your head and on or into a physical medium.

Personally, I like to write out my desires or create artwork that represents the desire or end goal. Once you have this vision, cut the goal into two smaller goals. Then do it again. And again, and again, and again until you have divided the goal into small enough steps so that each step seems relatively achievable in perhaps even mundane ways.

Now, don't go overboard, if you start sigilizing or casting spells to brush your teeth or tie your shoes... Well, you get the picture.

When you reach a place where your goal has been sufficiently divided into smaller achievable goals, write each goal out onto a piece of paper or in a digital document and turn every single one of them into a sigil. Charge all of them, one after another, until they are all charged within one session of sigilization.

The ultimate goal here is to reduce the large goal to a set of smaller goals that already have a higher probability of happening. These would be our fully-loaded coin pushers that only need another coin to bring a windfall of coinage into your pocket.

Keep a list of all the goals you turned into sigils and keep it out of sight and out of mind for at least 2-4 months. Towards the end of that time period, open up the paper, and review all the mini-goals you sigilized for. Note which ones materialized and which ones did not.

Take the goals that did manifest and use those items to create a new vision of your mega goal. Once again, cut that goal into smaller easier to accomplish mini-goals and sigilize each of them.

Charge all of the new mini-goals, one after another and again, keep a list of all the goals out of sight and out of mind. In another 2-4 months, review the document and note which goals manifested and which did not.

Repeat this process throughout the year and take notes on your progress as time goes on.

If done correctly, you will notice that many of the smaller goals manifest, paving the way for your larger goal to do the same. Take note of which sigilized goals worked best as far as how you worded the desire, how it manifested, and what dynamics are repeatable for those that worked well.

This process should eventually result in the manifestation of your mega-goal, while simultaneously creating new mega and mini goals as the process progresses.

In the following section, I will give you an example of how I was able to utilize this process to manifest a dream job without getting a college degree. I will further explain how I was able to do this while getting international awareness for my work in multiple books, magazines, and newspapers, including the New York Times and a case study at Rutgers University.

Chapter 2: Egregores and Their Logos

I do not have a university degree; however, my work has been taught to university students. That has always been something I find useful as a retrospective. I started actively working chaos magic around the same time I had taken a role as the social media manager and member of the sales team for my for my company after moving up from my previous role in retail and the other odd jobs previously mentioned.

While educating myself on sales, advertising, and marketing simultaneously while practicing sigilization as explained by Gordon White, I found many interesting parallels between sigil magic, branding, and the creation and use of corporate logos.

To say that a logo is a sigil and vice versa is an obvious truth to those working both chaos magic and marketing paradigms. The main difference is that a logo is a symbol created to affect the masses, where a sigil is designed to affect your subconscious mind alone.

The color psychology that goes into choosing the colors of a logo and the various branded assets such as business cards, brochures, white papers, websites, and the related digital content has a striking resemblance to the psychology of magical processes such as candle magic and the color system associated with spirits such as Santa Muerte.

The realization that marketing and advertising are a form of magic is a common byproduct of studying both. The yellow and red hues of McDonald's golden arches are literally designed with color theory to induce hunger when seen by human eyes.

The simplicity of Nike's black swoosh on a white background communicates both an aesthetic and a lifestyle. The three sixes in the Disney signature that evoke Satan... ok, well maybe that's going a bit too far into conspiracy territory but, you get the point.

The combination of symbols and colors used by the world's largest corporations are, in fact, sigil magic. Whether you realize it or not, these symbols and colors have a significant effect on all consumers, myself included.

If you think this does not apply to you, take a look at the products you buy and the companies that own the products... See any consistency? Right.

Modern human beings in westernized countries have minds that are saturated with corporate logos and brand identities which are based upon the data collected from people's purchases, online activity, and real-world physical interactions with brick and mortar establishments.

When beginning to do sigil magic for yourself and using this technology to better your life, it starts to become frighteningly obvious that (often dark) magic is being used on you by certain corporations on a daily basis.

After all, corporations themselves have personhood in America. Ultimately, they are egregores that feast upon our capitalist society—feeding not only upon our money but also our psychic energy, attention, and emotions.

Wait, what is an Egregore?

An egregore is an artificial psychic entity that is created and sustained by the people who support and believe in the entity, and it's alleged powers or dominion—for example, Santa Clause, YHVH.

So how do you, as the budding magician and marketing professional, leverage the magic of mega-corporations?

Starting with the sigilization technique above, you need to figure out what YOU really want in life. Not what your parents, priests, friends, or family expect of you, but what **you truly want**. The life that is a representation of your deepest joy.

Most of you reading this probably already have an idea in your head of what that looks like. Breaking that picture down into smaller goals and sigilizing it in the way described above is an excellent way to get your mojo working.

But, once you have begun this process, what do you do next?

Potential Applications for sigils:

- Embed them in the design of your company's logo
- Embed white sigils on the white space in your emails
- Draw them on the back of business cards and leave them in unique places in coffee shops, restaurants, hotels, convention centers, etc.
- Leave sheets of paper with nothing but a sigil and a QR code linked to branded content associated with the manifestation of the desire the sigil represents. Be sure to include a CTA.
- Embed sigils behind banner designs in blog posts and advertisements.

Conjuring Social Engagement

While your sigils are simmering in your unconscious mind (or in the mind of others when properly deployed) they should be working to manifest smaller goals that will result in the ultimate manifestation of your larger dreams. Which means, you have some work to do...

As a marketing professional, you need to bring awareness about your company and/or the companies of your clients to the masses. Analytics, social media monitoring platforms, email campaigns, reports, data collection, CRM, SEO, SEM, video, podcasts, webinars... These are the well-known mundane tools of the trade for the modern marketer of which you have likely already implemented in some form or another.

But how does magic fit into this equation?

When trying to get attention for your client or your brand, the first thing you need to do is stand out from the crowd, particularly, your competitors.

I am of the opinion that in order to do this, you need to think way outside-of-the-box, take risks, and do things your competitors are not.

For me, prior to starting in social media, my challenge was to move up from the extremely stressful position of being tossed around my company while doing everything from landscaping to production to retail, when I had originally been hired to work as a graphic designer.

But alas, in an SMB, the ground floor often comes with many hats and lower wages.

Again, that is where I found myself at the age of 21 in the summer of 2006. For the first three years, I did everything from mowing laws to refilling inkjets, from running a retail store to occasionally doing graphic design (the job I was hired for).

During those three years, I was moved around various odd jobs within the business and provided with little training for the majority of the work I was doing. I struggled with the high expectations that I should succeed in such an environment and was desperate to move up to something more secure, more focused, and more fulfilling within the company.

Having worked with various social media channels for the marketing of my band, I realized my company did not have anything going on in the space of social media. I decided I would approach the president of the company and make a case for us to get involved in social media marketing with me as the social media manager for the company.

First, I charged multiple sigils that pertained to obtaining the opportunity to do this work and to be put in charge of the company's social media efforts.

I then asked for a meeting with my president and, upon acquiring 10 minutes of his time, made my case that the company needed to get involved in social media as it was going to be a big deal in the B2B sector. Now, this was back in 2009, and there were virtually no case studies of social media as a viable marketing ploy for companies focused on a business to business paradigm.

I made my case to get involved in what I called "the big 4" - Facebook, Twitter, LinkedIn, and YouTube. I used examples from large B2C companies like Coca-Cola, Microsoft, and other companies of those sizes.

My president said that I would have to put on a full presentation for the C level executives of the company, which included our sales manager, CFO, CEO, and marketing manager (my boss at the time).

So, I spent a week with PowerPoint and made a demonstration that would relay all the information I had just reviewed with my president. Next, I put on a twenty-minute presentation in our board room for our C level employees as requested.

At the end of the meeting, I was met with mostly blank stares but, my president saw something in my determination. You have six months and zero budget, he said with a smile. If you can show some real return on investment, you will be our new social media manager.

I immediately got to work....

Destroy Your Printer

After that meeting, I sat at my desk, brainstorming ideas to leverage social media to increase brand awareness and generate sales. My biggest challenge was the zero-dollar budget. With no funds to invest, paid ads were out of the question, as was any content generation tools came with more than a zero-dollar price tag.

I thought long and hard about our customers and our products and started to focus on what the major pain points of our clients must be. That is when I heard one of my co-workers swearing under their breath, frustratingly trying to remove a paper jam from our central office copier.

That's it, I thought to myself! A contest! A video contest. **The Destroy Your Printer Contest!**

Now, believe it or not, I had not seen the movie "Office Space" at this point in time. But, I would certainly hear a lot more about film in the coming months. I wrote down an outline for the idea that had just popped into my head.

It all came together in about twenty minutes. My idea was to host a contest that would invite people to humorously and creatively destroy a troublesome printer in their office and get it on video. We would post the videos to our company blog, which would also feature a post inviting people to enter the contest. The winning contestant would win a prize for the best/funniest video.

I pitched the idea to management, and while the marketing manager was not totally on board, the president loved it and gave me permission to start a blogger hosted blog and set up social pages for our company on Facebook, Twitter, and LinkedIn.

Once I had the blog and initial post outlining the rules and deadline for the contest, I shared it via the company social media pages after sending out invites on my own social media pages. I invited friends, family, and co-workers to share the content on their social channels as well.

The contest was set to run for 6 months.

After four months of promoting the contest, we started getting submissions with a total of 6 submissions for the first contest (it eventually became an annual event).

The videos featured people using various tools to destroy their much-maligned printing devices—sledgehammers, baseball bats, bow and arrows, and most notably, explosives. The videos were hilarious, and word started spreading around the internet.

While all this was being done on a mundane level, I was simultaneously working on a magical one. Every day, I was sigilizing for success at each stage of the project. A sigil was created and charged for the success of the contest as well as each individual video and the viral sharing of said content.

I also created multiple sigils for the securing of the position of social media manager. Some of these sigils were placed into abstract pieces of artwork in my cubicle, or on the wall outside of it. As sigils need to be charged with psychic energy, displaying them drew the curiosity of my fellow employees. When they visited my area, I was able to harvest the energy generated by their curiosity, which helped to charge the sigils contained within the artwork.

One day, Mark Schaefer of the now world-famous {GROW} Marketing blog, wrote a glowing review of my contest, referring to it as "genius." At the time, I had no idea who Mark was, but I reached out and thanked him for the article and joined the mailing list for his blog. I was now a member of the ever-growing community of readers that were flocking to his phenomenal content.

From there, things just kind of exploded. I was contacted by an international trade publication who wanted to run a story about my contest. Thanks to that initial article and video on The Recycler Magazine's website, I would go on to become a regular contributor to the periodical.

I even penned a cover article about my company, which resulted in international brand awareness for the business. Next, the New York Times reached out and wrote an article on their small business blog about the contest. This garnered me a lot of attention from the upper echelon of social media influencers and professionals from around the world.

My work and I ended up being featured in multiple social media books, including "No Bullshit Social Media," Return on Influence," and "Visual Marketing." The exposure from all of this international press then resulted in my work being featured as part of the curriculum for the first two years of the Social Media MBA program at Rutgers University.

The contest was hailed as one of the first viable B2B social media success stories with a proven return on investment. It ran annually for five years and resulted in multiple new clients, including a larger contract with an international fiber optics company called OFS-Fitel, a client that is still a dedicated customer to my former company to this day.

Needless to say, by the end of the first contest, I was awarded the position of Chief Social Media Marketing Engineer" at my company. For over ten years, I lead the company through multiple out of the box and truly creative marketing campaigns while simultaneously working as a member of the sales team. I managed to close hundreds of thousands of dollars in sales in contract, retail, and machine sales alike, many of which I garnered through the sharing of the content generated by the contest.

Between the actions put into the mundane side of the contest in conjunction with my on-going sigilization work, I was able to connect each of the smaller goals within the framework of the larger goal (becoming the social media manager) and manifest the desire within 6 months.

Chapter 3: Hyper-Sigils and Servitors

Sigils are both simple to create and easy to deploy. They are also a very potent form of magic, but they are not the sum of a complete magical practice. Spells, enchantments, and rituals come in all shapes and sizes from all over the world. Every culture has its own form of magic and metaphysical practices. Of course, each of these cultures also has its own type of spellcraft.

For me personally, when it comes to spellcraft, I lean heavily on the technologies of conjure (also known as hoodoo or rootwork). While there are thousands of spells to choose from within various traditions from all over the earth, I prefer those of conjure for several reasons.

First, the spells of conjure and hoodoo rely upon physical materials such as dirt, powder, herbs, stones, incense, candles, and other physical items. Unlike some enchantments that only utilize words or energy, the spells of folk magic use physical objects and links in conjunction with spirits to manifest magical results.

This positively resonates with me for multiple reasons and allows me to invest more of myself into the work than spells that rest solely upon energy, psychology and/or spirit.

I studied the western esoteric tradition and magical systems from various cultures for about a decade before I lit my first candle and charged my first sigil. And while I had been able to teach myself a lot through books, and trial and error, like all crafts, magic is best learned from a teacher.

After looking at various online courses in the mystical arts, I settled upon Jason Miller's Strategic Sorcery course. Jason, an initiate of several magical lodges, Tibetan Buddhism, and other systems of advanced magical training, offered a one-year correspondence course.

As previously mentioned, the course cost $150.00. While I could have scrounged and saved for it, I wanted to test out my own magical skills to see if I could acquire the course without having to pay for it.

After thinking about a few different ways to achieve the goal, I decided to try to get my company to foot the bill as I would be using much of the content of the course to help land more sales and increase the ROI of the marketing department.

I charged a shoal of sigils, each with a variation of the intent being to get my boss to approve my course as a company expense.

When trying to figure out how I would sell him on the idea, I decided to take a considerable risk.

As he knew that I was interested in the magical arts, metaphysics, and spirituality, I could tell he was curious about my ideas. He himself seemed open to things such a Buddhism and philosophy. I asked for the opportunity to do a short fifteen-minute presentation for him in our board room about chaos magic, emphasizing the art of sigilization and how it can be applied to marketing and sales.

To my great delight, he accepted my presentation a couple days later. I relayed all the information above, showing him how to create and charge sigils while drawing comparisons to the creation and deployment of corporate logos. I shared my ideas on color theory and advertising and how there is an obvious crossover between the psychology of magic and the art of advertising.

At the end of my presentation, I expressed great interest in bettering my understanding of how magical technologies could be used in successful marketing and sales campaigns and made my case for the strategic sorcery course.

When I finished, he thought silently for about a minute, reviewing the presentation in his head while looking at the examples, notes, and diagrams I had drawn on the whiteboard during my presentation.

I can see the value in this, he said with a smile; as a business expense, one hundred and fifty dollars is not much at all; just sign up for the course today, and I will have our finance department cut you a check for the cost.

I thanked him and expressed my genuine gratitude for the opportunity to not only take the course but to be able to leverage the wisdom within and apply it to my efforts in the arts of marketing and sales.

This process of using a presentation on how magic works as part of a magical working to achieve the end goal of getting the cost of a course on sorcery covered by my employer is an excellent place to move onto a new concept called the "hypersigil."

What Is a Hypersigil?

A hypersigil is any creative work of fiction (novel, poem, song, film, video game, animation, drawing, painting, etc.) that is created in a state of gnosis and approached as a highly charged magical ritual. The intent of this ritual being that your creation brings forth the desired narrative as a direct script for reality to follow in which your desire is made manifest.

Essentially, a hypersigil is the writing of a story. It is the story of the life you desire or the things and experiences that you most desperately want. A successful hypersigil will result in the fictional narrative coming to fruition in your life as closely as possible to the events of the fictional story.

The most famous example of a successful hypersigil is legendary comic book author Grant Morrison's epic comic book series "The Invisibles." This particularly obscure but cult classic of comic book genius was largely the source material for the much better-known film "The Matrix."

It is well known that the Wachowski sisters borrowed so heavily from Grant's masterpiece that they literally had various issues of the Invisibles laying around the set of the film, from which, they borrowed heavily for their own dystopian science fiction masterpiece.

Unlike the film, which, while a smash hit, pales in comparison to the source material from which they so carefully borrowed from, The Invisibles is a hypersigil that, while starting with a dystopian feel, is a masterful ritual created to cause the fertile soil for the very antithesis of such an event.

Which is to say, it was created to bring about a better world from the ashes of chaos and also, perhaps more importantly for Grant, to turn himself into a world-famous writer whose work would go on to touch some of the greatest comic book narratives and characters in the history of the world.

Grant wrote himself into the story as a character and super/anti-hero type badass called "King Mob." Grant has famously warned that both good and ill put into the context of your hypersigil (if done correctly and with great potency) will manifest in your life.

It is a well known and somewhat terrifying fact that as Grant wrote Kin Mob's narrative in one part of the series in which the character becomes extremely sick with various horrible symptoms. This was followed by Grant himself suddenly becoming extremely sick and ending up in the hospital. The doctors could not figure out what he had and Grant came potentially close to death.

However, he continued to write King Mob's story in which the character eventually was able to rest, recuperate, heal, and become stronger than ever before. Shortly after this part of the narrative was written by Grant, he made a miraculous recovery.

In this respect, it is essential to understand that a hypersigil has the potential to manifest whatever it is you put into the creative process, including ultimately harmful and destructive things. With that in mind, it would be wise to only write positive elements into a hypersigil that is directed to change the lives of you, your family, friends and/or loved ones.

Servitors: The Mascots of Spirits

When it comes to using spirits to bring your business success, some of the most potent and useful entities you can summon and work with are those of which you create yourself. Servitors are essentially synthetic spirits that are created by giving them a symbol, name, and program.

To program a servitor, a set of qualities that are conducive to the goals you want the servitor to meet or exceed are given to the created entity, and then it is sent to work on fulfilling its programming.

I refer to servitors as "the mascots of spirits" because, in a way, that is precisely what they are. A mascot, whether it be for a sports team or a spokesperson for a product or company, have long been used in advertising to entertain and entice consumer participation with a brand. This is specifically done in order to get people to purchase the brand's products.

Examples of traditional mascots would include The Boston Red Sox Mascot "Wally," the Geico Gecko, and Tony the Tiger. Chances are, you are able to think of various other mascots that you have encountered in your life.

When it comes to servitors, they are not unlike mascots in that they embody the elements desired by their creators and owners and are ultimately set to work by giving them skills and character traits that will attract a targeted audience or continually work to achieve a specific goal, such as helping you to quit smoking or assisting you in getting a job interview.

Like organic or traditional spirits such as gods, goddesses, angels, and so on, servitors will require offerings and creative energy invested into them to stay energized. In this respect, properly "feeding" your servitors will allow them to be able to assist you in fulfilling your dreams which is in part the servitor's responsibility to manifest.

As for what to offer to the spirit to keep it "fed," you are the one who has created and given the entity "life," you should be able to decide what would be best for offerings. If you are unsure, simply ask the servitor a question and let your imagination open to what you think the response would be. Once you have gotten to know your servitor better, you will be able to provide it with the proper offerings and energy to keep it going and working to fulfill its role in helping you reach your goal.

Servitor Case Study #1: Jabooda

Jabooda is the name of the band that I played in and toured with throughout Northeastern USA for about a decade between 2006 and 2017. During the time of the band, we worked hard, practiced often, and began playing shows at any venue that would take us.

What started mostly as gigs in friend's backyards and massive house parties eventually lead to local and regional bars and before long, larger night clubs and eventually sizeable music festivals.

At around the three-year mark, I began experimenting with ideas for guerilla marketing campaigns for the band and ultimately decided upon the following.

I printed up several thousand stickers on waterproof, ultra-sticky and virtually impossible to remove custom made adhesive stock paper. The message simple read, "What is Jabooda"? No URL, no indication of what Jabooda actually was, no names of band members, NOTHING else except "What is Jabooda"?

These stickers were distributed via our fans, friends and family members in addition to each member of the band also putting these stickers up where ever we felt like putting them up.

We did this for about a year before producing a second version of the stickers that were identical to the first stickers, but now also having a tiny URL to our Facebook page. Once again, we distributed the stickers to hundreds of people at show after show over the course of the next two years.

Many of the second-generation stickers ended up in close proximity to the first-generation stickers and from there, continued to pop up randomly in places all over the United States. The second generation of stickers however, brought a lot more people to our website, generating lots of email contacts from people inquiring to know WHAT IS JABOODA?

We decided to expedite the process of exposure for our questionable stickers, and a plan was suggested by my bass player Travis Sweny. At the time, Travis and his brothers worked at a FedEx hub in CT, loading and unloading tractor-trailer trucks in a warehouse. Travis's idea was to plaster the inside of each and every truck with the second-generation stickers. Which, of course, we did.

Within a few weeks we were getting emails and messages from other people at FedEx hubs from all over the country. Many of the folks who reached out, became fans of the band and listened to our music, telling others about the mysterious stickers and the band who was ultimately behind them.

During this time, we would hand these stickers out to our fans at shows for free, and slowly, over the next three years, the stickers started popping up all over the place. Next, we started seeing posts on social media from people several states away talking about how the stickers had found their way to places like New York City, Province Town, San Francisco, and various random cities and small towns all over the USA.

Eventually, we started seeing photographs of our stickers in European countries such as Amsterdam and Spain. This was in part due to getting interviewed by social media marketing legend, Mark Schaefer. As previously mentioned, Mark had been kind enough to write an article about the destroy your printer contest.

After that, we stayed in touch and became friends, and one day he offered a call for guest posts on his {GROW} Marketing blog. I submitted the story about the stickers and the FedEx hub, and Mark absolutely loved the concept and published a guest post I wrote about our efforts on his blog.

The blog post in question has been posted here in its entirety in for your consideration:

Guerrilla marketing is about eclectic combinations of music, mystery, art, culture, humor and social dynamics coming together into a sales pitch that doesn't appear to be a sales pitch. It manifests itself as a hip invitation to join or to be part of a movement.

One of the most infamous recent examples of guerrilla marketing was when the adult swim Network[1] placed electronic signs for its Aqua Teen

Hunger Force show around Boston, resulting in a bomb scare and eventual arrests. It didn't work, but you get the idea. I've had to resort to guerrilla tactics myself in my job with Expert Laser Services[2], primarily because I needed to sell more stuff, but had no money for marketing. I had to get inventive. I had to get guerrilla.

An idea sprang from my own frustrations of having to deal with office laser printers and copiers which simply didn't work when you needed them most. In fact, I genuinely developed a hatred for certain pieces of office equipment.

Through Twitter, blogs, Facebook and LinkedIn, I promoted a contest that would award a small prize to the video depicting the most creative destruction of a printer. People blew them up, tossed them out of windows and crushed them with a backhoe. In essence, the social web was providing my content. Remember, I had no budget!

Soon, the project was featured all over the web and was the top video story in an online trade magazine for several consecutive weeks. We actually generated sales leads and new customers from this promotion.

But the most fun guerrilla social media tactic had nothing to do with business, it involved my band, Jabooda.

When the band formed four years ago, I produced several thousand stickers that read "What is Jabooda?" Through friends of friends of friends, these stickers made it on to random spots throughout the United States and even Europe.

When we came out with the second generation of stickers I included a small URL on each one to help people connect with us on the web. In addition to hitting the streets with the sticker, we got guerrilla with the distribution process, too.

Two of the guys from the band worked for FedEx and started to put a supply of stickers in every truck they unloaded or loaded. Over the course of the year "what is Jabooda" became a bit of a sensation and we gained new

---

1.   http://www.adultswim.com/

2.   http://www.expertlaserservices.com/

fans at FedEx hubs in nearly every state and many countries around the world. FedEx had become our own personal social media network!

The stickers drove people to our website where we were able to collect names for our mailing list.

About two years ago some of our new fans built a page on Facebook to lobby to get us on the bill at the Wormtown Music Festival, one of New England's longest-running and most popular music events. We did not get the slot, but we were moving in the right direction.

The following year the competition heated up and Facebook alone wasn't going to do it. To get into Wormtown's Strangecreek festival lineup the next year, we had to win a battle of the bands competition. We actually made it to the finals but to win, part of the criteria was the size of our fan base. It was time to use that mailing list!

We got the word out to all those crazy Jabooda fans and were able to attract a large crowd from several different states. In fact, it was the largest crowd of the night and we won, securing our place on the festival bill.

Don't have a marketing budget? Don't let it get you down. Go guerrilla!

The combined exposure from the stickers, the shows, and the article that Mark kindly let me publish on his extremely popular marketing blog lead to thousands of people reaching out. Many of these people voted for our band for a battle of the bands which garnered us several gigs for some large music festivals, but, that was just the beginning.

With all the dynamics and energy we had been able to produce around Jabooda, I decided to create a sigil that would embody the spirit of this magical thing that we had manifested and enliven the sigil to become a servitor to help us to achieve a few bucket list items.

Namely, getting to share the stage with some legendary musicians from bands like The Allman Bros, The Grateful Dead, Big Brother and the Holding Company, and Blues Legend Johnny Winter. All goals of which, we eventually achieved.

The symbol was created with the traditional formulation of a sigil based upon the name of the band sans removing the vowels. The repeating letters were removed, and the remaining letters in JABOODA were rearranged into a glyph that would represent the band. The final product was a symbolic representation of the band, the fans, the music, and the phenomena that we were able to bring about with the stickers and the FedEx operation.

The symbol became present at shows, on t-shirts, projected on to screens behind the stage, added to stickers and social media channels, and it just became ubiquitous as a visual representation of the group as well as the question, "What is Jabooda" and the answers each member of our community had to that to particular question.

As this sigil embedded itself into the iconography of our live performances, every show began to become an offering to the servitor. Every song, every cheer from the fans, every light show, the mingling scent of beer, marijuana, and tobacco smoke, it all combined into a musical ritual setting in which the servitor known as Jabooda would feast upon the joyous release that was the majority of shows we put on.

After a few years of these ritual offerings in the guise of concerts, I could tell that the servitor had become a potent synthetic entity, and I decided to start working with it much in the same way that you would with an organic spirit or deity.

On one specific occasion, we had been trying and failing to book a particular club of renown within our scene, and I decided to do an evocation of the servitor using a blend of evocation techniques that combined elements of goetic and hoodoo/conjure technologies.

I followed the same protocols used to evoke a goetic spirit (as laid out for this hybrid system of evocation of which was designed by The Queen of Pentacles[3]), but rather than use a sigil for a goetic entity, I used the sigil I created to represent my servitor Jabooda.

Through the steps outlined above, I performed the evocation exactly as outlined with a few minor alterations to better fit my servitor (I chanted a verse from one of the band's songs in lieu of an enn).

---

3.   http://queenofpentaclesconjure.blogspot.com/2011/05/conjure-with-goetia.html

The Sigil of Jabooda

The request made to the spirit was to intervene on our behalf to the owners of the desired club with the aim of the enchantment to get their attention and interest and assist in getting us a show at the venue.

I decide to do this particular working as up to that point in time, we had not been able to get into this night club, and I wanted to see if we could metaphysically and or psychologically "grease the wheels," so to speak.

Just being able to add the name of this club to our resume of venues performed at was a massive feather in our cap and a potent tool to help us continue getting into bigger and better clubs.

Within a week or so of doing this work, we spoke to the management of the venue and were easily able to secure a gig, something of which prior to this project, had proven to be almost impossible.

Servitor Case Study #2: Expert Laser Man

At the same time I was experimenting with a servitor to serve the success of my band, I was simultaneously working on building a potent servitor to help build global brand awareness for my company and to assist in bringing in SQLs and funding for larger marketing initiatives.

This process was quite different from the creation of the Jabooda servitor and leaned heavily upon the use of storytelling, narrative, pop culture magic, and modern entertainment tropes.

As previously mentioned, Expert Laser Man is a fictional character that I developed to act as a servitor that would build global brand awareness and drive new sales for my company. The idea for the character was partly inspired by the destroy your printer contest, specifically contestant Eric Morse's epic car jump video[4], which took the prize for that year's contest.

That particular video made me think about the heroic jump that Eric was able to accomplish in his printer destruction video. I thought, what if there was a comic-book style superhero called "Expert Laser Man."

In order to create and release this servitor, I needed to develop a back story and personal mythos for Expert Laser Man. Who was he? What did he do? How do I make him a hero?

The first part of this equation was fulfilled by making a faux movie trailer of which I tried to emulate the MARVEL studios style film trailers for the marvel cinematic universe.

To do this, I wrote a script. I used stock footage to create a story in which a heroic mystery man called "Expert Laser Man" rebelled against artificial intelligence that had infected copiers worldwide and resulted in a terminator style attack of the machines type of narrative.

The video first got the attention of Recycler Magazine, which did a story about the character. This helped to make the character go viral within our industry, which laid the groundwork for a very exciting expansion of Expert Laser Man's fictional universe.

4.		https://www.youtube.com/watch?v=JzYFjCk6sMk

Around the time of the Recycler Magazine article, a large OEM in the copier industry had recently become a corporate partner to our business. They took great interest in my out-of-the-box approach to generating digital marketing content, namely, the Expert Laser Man Video.

They brought me in for a meeting and asked if I had any other creative ideas in the same vein as the video.

I immediately pitched an idea I had been sitting on for years, which was an "Expert Laser Man" Video game. In the game, the protagonist could be played as a laser baring heroic IT man who bravely saves his co-workers from the evil artificial intelligence riddled printers and copiers who had become sentient and bloodthirsty.

They instantly loved the idea and within a few days, gave me $10,000 to fund the project. I created and produced the game with my partners from the Gorilla Tactics video game studio out of Amherst, MA, and also subsequently recorded the soundtrack for the game.

With the help of Guerilla Tactics, I was able to bring the game to life. In order to incentivize people to play the game and subsequently become a marketing qualified lead, we enticed players by offering unlimited entry to a sweepstakes in which the winner would garner a $500 cash prize.

Players could enter the contest every time they beat the game, which kept them coming back for more and more. The game was specifically targeted to IT professionals (many of which are gamers) who were the primary buyer persona that we were going after in order to create sales qualified leads.

We ended up generating hundreds of MQLs, which again, drew deeper curiosity from our corporate partner who, after seeing the results of the game, gave me an additional $21,000 for marketing campaigns, one of which, would continue the fictional legend of Expert Laser Man.

Chapter 4: The Process of Magic in the Art of Sales

When applying the process of magic to the art of sales, there are many different applications from many different cultures and traditions throughout the world. In this chapter, I am going to introduce some of the various dynamics and types of magic that can be applied to both sales and marketing to help increase the success of both endeavors.

Synthetic Spirits, Buyer Personas and Egregores

In the gigantic world of magic, there are hundreds of thousands of gods, spirits, angels, demons, demi-gods, and entities of all shapes and sizes.

Every culture of the world has its spirits of which the people of said culture interact with in some way. Some people believe in spirits, some don't. Before we go any further, I would like to point out an important fact. You do not need to believe in spirits in order to "work" with them. I myself, am an agnostic and do not necessarily believe in spirits, nor do I totally deny they exist.

But even if I were an atheist, that would not matter. If you reduce magic to a purely psychological practice, it still works. While I tend to view magic primarily through the meta-model, I still work with spirits regardless of whether I believe in them or not. I believe that most spirits are powerful ancient egregores.

If nothing else, they represent the concentration of power for specialized effects made manifest in anthropometric personalities. Every spirit, god, angel, etc., can be viewed as a specialized professional useful for specific tasks.

For example...

Need something in a hurry? Try Saint Expedite. Want to catch a fish? Talk to Poseidon. Looking to cause some trouble, call Loki...

But how exactly do you "work" with a god or spirit, especially if you do not believe they exist? It may seem trivial at first, but to work with a spirit, you need to create a relationship with them.

Just like people, you have to get to know someone before you are able to enter into a working relationship. And, just like real relationships with other human beings, there is a give and take in these situations. No one likes to work for free.

So how do you start a relationship with spirit? First, you do research about them.

Let's say you are looking to go on a long journey and you want to find the best deals on hotels, the quickest and safest routes to each location, and also enjoy some beautiful scenery along the way, all while keeping things within budget and also avoiding issues like flat tires or speeding tickets.

In this case, the Greek god Hermes (or Mercury as he is known in the Roman pantheon), would be an excellent choice. Why? Well because...

"As the god of boundaries and transitions, Hermes was known to be quick and cunning and had the ability to freely move between the mortal and divine worlds. It is this skill that made him a luck-bringing messenger to the gods and intercessor between mortals and the divine.

He is also the patron and protector of travelers, herdsmen, thieves, orators and wit, literature and poets, athletics and sports, invention and trade. *In some myths, Hermes is also depicted as a trickster where he would outwit the gods either for the good of humankind or for his own personal amusement and satisfaction." - greekgodsandgoddesses.net*

Indeed, Hermes possess many of the skills that would be useful when planning and executing the trip mentioned above, but how do you utilize a spirit (or if you do not believe in spirits, an egregore) to help you in a real life endeavor?

Like any real-life relationship, it starts with an introduction. When it comes to spirits, rather than a handshake, the making of offerings is generally the first step in developing and keeping a relationship with a spirit/egregore.

Traditionally, making offerings to gain the attention and hopefully, the favor of a spirit is fairly easy. A small table or space on a shelf will be needed upon which you would place an image of the spirit, a glass of spring water, a candle, and perhaps some incense.

Light the candle and incense, look at the image, and say something to the effect of...

Greetings, Hermes. I (insert name) seek your assistance in the planning and execution of a journey to (location). I am looking to get the best deals on hotels, the most excellent rental car possible while avoiding trouble and calamity of all kinds, particularly speeding tickets, car troubles, and traffic.

In return for these services rendered, I will repay the favor by offering you (insert items). I make this offering of incense, water, flame, and prayer and ask of you these things in kindness and respect, amen/so mote it be.

If you would like to be more formal, you could start your prayer above with an orphic hymn dedicated to Hermes as these ancient prayers are loaded with power from thousands of years of use.

Now, while the above is a perfectly traditional way of making an offering to a spirit you wish to employ to help in achieving your goals, it is only one way of making offerings, and many business owners use more modern means to achieve the same goal.

For example, Christian owned companies may pay homage to Jesus by printing a prayer from the bible on the side of all their tractor-trailer trucks, the prayers being read by thousands of people on the highways while their products are being shipped.

Some companies incorporate the image of the spirit in their company logo, such as the spread eagle siren, which adorns all the products sold by Starbucks, or the Roman goddess Libertas as seen in branding for companies such as Liberty Mutual.

Incorporating the name, image, and mythos of a spirit into the branding of your company acts as a potent offering to the spirit. In turn, these offerings will often help to manifest the goals of which you have petitioned said spirit to assist with.

Spirits for Sales And Marketing

Now, when it comes to sales, there is a plethora of gods, spirits, deities, and entities to choose from in regard to the acquisition of financial wealth, but when it comes right down to it, you would be hard-pressed to find one more powerful or responsive than Jupiter.

Jupiter, king of the Roman pantheon of gods, is the epitome of power and wealth. Whether you consider him a real god capable of bestowing riches upon you or merely a symbolic representation of the wealth and power you hope to obtain, working with this particular spirit has, in my practice, proven to be a phenomenal boon to my own success.

From closing sales to attracting leads and growing commissions, he is easy to approach, and if honored and respected, his blessings are often profound and immense. Experiment with offerings of different types on a daily basis such as those mentioned above and/or in conjunction with the reading of orphic hymns dedicated to his glory.

If he comes through in assisting your goals as petitioned, give public thanks to him. This can be done in the real world, social media, etc.

Something to the effect of **"Hail Jove! Thanks be to the king of the Gods!"** would be a good start. If anyone takes notice of your giving thanks and asks for an explanation, go on to give him a referral like you would anyone else who comes through for you.

Customer-Centric Spirit Offerings

The spirits that are important to you as a business owner are one thing. The spirits that are important to your customers are another thing entirely. When I use the term spirits, it does not have to be in reference to a spiritual or religious entity.

As previously mentioned, corporations are essentially modern synthetic spirits. This can be a useful perspective to understand when thinking about how to invoke or evoke the spirits that your customers work with or are fans of.

Think about it, if you know that your customers like to drink a certain brand of cola, would it not make sense to research that brand and feed your customers offerings that align with that brand and the synthetic spirit that it represents?

Creating buyer personas based upon the real and synthetic spirits that your customers love and interact with is an excellent way to infuse your marketing and sales efforts with correspondences that relate to their emotional attachment to that brand or spirit.

By evoking the same techniques that your consumer's other favorite brands exemplify, you can transmute that data into useful enchantments that will attract, delight, and encourage your customers. From there, you can create entertaining and educational content that provides value to them.

In this way, you are making emotional and, in some cases, spiritual offerings directly to your clients, whether they are aware of this or not. From the mundane perspective, this could be something as simple as studying the other brands your consumers love through polling initiatives and then putting the same tactics of those brands into your marketing and sales protocols.

From a spiritual perspective, this could mean understanding the spiritual dynamics of your consumer base and infusing your marketing and sales materials and content with symbolic representations of those things which they hold sacred, thus infusing your service to them as a brand whom they choose to do business with in a deeper more spiritual way.

For example, there is a large metalhead/goth subculture that is one of the the target markets of Monster energy drinks. While this was initially the case due to the fact that said brand was likely targeting those specific dynamics with their branding and aesthetic, it was taken to another level when a well-meaning Christian woman launched an attack campaign against the brand as being literally satanic (which of course, is not true, despite her claims).

While this woman is on a literal modern-day crusade to dismantle and ultimately destroy the monster energy drink brand, she has accomplished quite the opposite (much to the joy of monster energy).

Her massively viral videos attempt to string false correlations between the logo of the monster energy drink brand and connect them to ancient Jewish language dynamics and gematria. She claims the brands iconic "monster slash" is, in fact, three letters from the Jewish alphabet that each have a numeric value of six which in turn would equate to 666...

With the monster slash being composed of three slashes which vaguely (at best) resemble the Jewish characters she claims they actually are, she attempts to suggest the logo is a cleverly hidden satanic message.

Now, while her claims are wildly unfounded and have been proven time and again to be false, her insane attack against monster energy has helped to grow support from atheists, Satanists, occultists, Wiccans, witches, and other types of people who identify with the very thing she is fighting against.

The "negative" press she was trying to create ultimately boosted sales for the energy drink empire and greatly expanded the very company she was trying to destroy. Monster's ability to transmute the attacks against their brand and leverage it as free advertising, which resulted in millions of dollars in sales, is an absolute testament to the power of using literal and, in this case, "fake" magic to turn a major profit.

It is perhaps one of the best-case studies in modern marketing about how to use the magic of religion, spirituality, symbols, and pop-culture to create a massively successful brand that literally feeds off of their opponent's attempts to take them down.

Digital VS Material Sales Sorcery

When it comes to using magical tech in sales, you can largely divide many of the most effective tactics into two groups. Digital Magic and Material Magic. The first relies upon embedding magical words, sigils, colors, numbers, symbols, and other magical tools into your everyday mundane emails, social interactions, and snail-mail campaigns.

The latter touches upon using material-based magical tools such as documents, signatures, photographs, business cards, brochures, powders, oils, candles, and other magical and mundane physical objects.

For an example of a digital form of practical sales sorcery, consider one of the most seen dynamics of your personal brand. Your email signature.

The email e-signature is an often overlooked and underused yet rather potent space for marketing and personal branding. There are enormous opportunities for using this small space to drive traffic to your website and enchant your communications for better movement through the buyer's journey and sales pipeline.

One of the techniques that I used over the twelve years I worked in corporate sales was embedding sigils into emails in my signature, either openly as part of a graphical design element, or hidden in a JPEG behind a blank white block so that while the sigil was actually in the file, it was invisible to the naked eye.

The sigils created for this purpose would be a statement of desire being charged from the prospective client's perspective. For example, "I am going to buy "X" number of copiers in the second quarter of this year from Nathan's company."

The brain states produced while working on a computer and staring at a screen for 9 hours a day is conducive to a minor trance-like state. When sigils are digested in this state, they can be implanted in the prospect's subconscious mind.

Over time and repetitions, you can track the success of the sigils based upon how many of which deals follow suit with the dynamics of the sigil. In regard to the last example, the client would, in fact, have bought the desired number of copiers from me by the end of the second quarter.

As for a material-based act of magic for success in sales endeavors, there are a host of different ways to enchant mundane items like paper documents, business cards, brochures, white papers, resumes, and various other office related documentation.

When it comes to manifesting your will upon another with the intent to get them to do something in your favor and for the betterment of your career, conjure oils and other hoodoo enchantments are a great option.

Different formulations that can help you to land your dream job, ensure you land large contracts and hardware sales, get a raise and/or a promotion and pretty much any other career goals you may have can be found in various magical manuals.

Now, let us say you are submitting your resume for a new job opportunity. While confident that you have all the necessary requirements and accolades to land the job, you still want to add a little mojo to help push your offering beyond those of the competing applications.

You could use a properly consecrated conjure oil to enhance the probability of getting your potential employer's attention. For example, by applying a small drop of command and control oil to each tip of each corner of your resume, you can increase the likelihood of selling them on hiring you.

Command and control oils are alleged to influence the person whom it is given to in that they are more likely to do what you would like them to do. Command and control oils are oils infused with herbs and stones which are them imbued with power by praying certain Christian prayers over the finished oil.

This could be supplemented with a sweeting spell of which can be done with a business card and/or a photo of your new employer, specifically the person who is in charge of interviewing and hiring you.

A sweeting spell is designed to impress a genuine and potent sense of likeability towards you from your hiring manager (or anyone of whom you are trying to get into the good graces of).

Here is my own recipe for a sweetening spell.

Required Materials:
Business Card and/or Photo
Empty Bowl
Blade
Honey or Maple Syrup
A Sweeting Sigil
Small Taper Candle (White)
Lavender
Cinquefoil
Luck Oil

First, you want to create or find a premade sweetening sigil (I would suggest using Jason Miller's sweetening glyph from financial sorcery if you are not confident about making your own). Draw the sigil on the back of your target's business card. If you have a photo of the person, draw the sigil on the front of their photo as well.

Place the card and/or the photograph face up in the bowl with the photograph on top (if you have one). Next, take the candle and use the blade to carve the target's name into the wax of the candle. Anoint the carved candle with some type of influence oil and sprinkle it with lavender and cinquefoil.

Light the candle and drop a few drops of wax on the photo and business card and then place the candle on the hot wax. Ensuring not to knock over the candle, pour honey or maple syrup into the bowl covering the photo and business card.

Optional: Recite a prayer to your spirit of choice for assistance in making the spell work or perhaps a mantra or song representing the manifestation of your desire. Let the candle burn out. Do not leave the burning candle unattended.

On the day of your interview, wear a dab of luck and success oil on your neck and dab your hands with command and control oil prior to sitting down for the interview.

Chapter 5: On Influencing Choices

When you get right down to it, sales and marketing are both about using the forces you have available to you to get people to purchase your products rather than another's.

In this respect, there are of course, the tactics of the old school nuclear family salesman. However, this is a dying art in our modern world where trust is paramount. These old school manipulation techniques are looked down upon with great scorn in our modern age.

That being said, influencing people is still a required ability for anyone who is honestly going to try their hand at a career in sales.

With that in mind, there are some very subtle techniques from both mundane and magical actions that can be used to affect the subconscious mind of buyers without their noticing.

Digital Color Manipulation

When writing emails, you have an excellent opportunity to plant seeds of intention in your customer's subconscious mind. For example, if you were to write the following email, your obvious intention may or may not come to fruition.

*Dear,*_____________

Hi _____________ ! I was just following up to see if you were at all interested in the brochure that I sent per your request last week. Whether or not you buy "insert product" from me, I would like to help you find the right vendor and product, even if you do not ultimately buy from us.

This email helps to build trust as you openly say that you want to help them get the right product even if they end up choosing another vendor. However, there is an opportunity here to influence the buyer in a practically invisible manner.

The eyes cannot always perceive subtle changes in the shade of a color, and yet, that information will still be recorded by the brain. So, if you take the same email and make the red text highlighted below a slightly lighter shade of black, you can implant an idea into your customer's subconscious mind in the same way that you would implant a sigil in your own.

To illustrate this, I am using red to highlight the targeted text.

Hi _______________ ! I was just following up to see if you were at all interested in the brochure that I sent per your request last week. Whether or not you buy "insert product" from me, I would like to help you find the right vendor and product, even if you do not ultimately buy from us.

By changing the color of the red text to a virtually identical but completely different shade of black, you will be able to insert this idea into the mind of the buyer without them realizing it.

In my own experience, I found that when I implemented this tactic in email conversations and compared them to those in which I did not use said tactic, I noticed that the deals with the color manipulation almost always closed sooner.

This can also be done in real-world conversations, on the phone, or through Zoom when speaking to a client by making a subtle change in your voice and putting the focus on the statement of intent.

When these tactics are combined with some form of command and control spell, you will find that the combination can be quite potent.

Command and control oil can be worn as a cologne on your hands or added to the corner of contracts and other financial documents that will ensure a long-term relationship with the client.

Furthermore, command and control oil can be used in spells to focus dominance on the sales process allowing you greater ability to affect the consumer's choice of product.

Here is a command and control spell of my own.

Required Materials:

Candle (preferably a human shaped candle, however, a plain white one will do just fine.)

Blade

Business Card

Dominance sigil

String

Command and Control Oil

Bowl

Start by carving the name of the potential buyer into the candle. Next, take the string and tie it around the candle. If using a person shaped candle, be sure that the string binds both hands.

Find a sigil used for dominance or create your own. Draw it over the front of the buyer's business card and place it in a bowl. Place the candle on top of the business card inside the bowl. If the candle will not stand on its own, affix it to the card with hot wax.

Anoint the candle with command and control oil. You may also want to sprinkle the anointed candle with herbs associated with control and dominance.

Light the candle and it let burn all the way down, also burning the business card. Do this the night before the final sales meeting with your client.

Etheric Snail Mail

The story behind this method of magical communication is steeped in humor and a bit of high wyrdness (spelling intentional).

As for the method itself, it is as follows: (The section below was previously published as a blog post)

Below you will find an experiment that I did for work and which I am also submitting to Jason Miller as a homework assignment for his STRATEGIC SORCERY[1] course (highly recommended). This was originally posted to Jason's web forum.

I thought that this may be a useful experiment for other sales/ marketing professionals and felt that it would be well received here on my blog.

Good morning everyone!

---

1.   http://www.inominandum.com/blog/strategic-sorcery-spring-sale-2/

I wanted to post a few magick experiments of my own, get some feedback and hopefully hear about some of your own work as well!

Experiment #1: Telepathy for Business Communications

I touched upon this work in another post and wanted to give a more detailed description here.

I work for a managed print services company as a sales consultant and I am also the social media marketing director for the same employer.

About a month and a half ago I contacted a prospect with the hope to garner the necessary information to propose a managed print contract for said prospect.

Basically, I generate a report about an organizations laser printer/ copier fleet and give that report to a prospect free of charge. Included in the report is a proposal showing how much consumables, repairs, and service would cost with our program versus how the company currently purchases those items.

I would say that eight out of ten times, I get the business of the prospect because our program saves our prospects a significant amount of time and money over their current vendor.

Sometimes however, prospects have already had a report done by a competitor, have done it themselves, or don't see the value in the paradigm shift from their current process.

This is what happened with a recent sale to a new prospect.

I called him and gave my elevator pitch. He sounded both annoyed and interested at the same time, explaining he had already done this report and was going to be meeting with two of our competitors the following day.

I asked if he could give me a list of the machines that he had so that I could generate a solid proposal. He basically said no, to which I told him, well, I can't give you a proposal without that information. He (sounding frustrated) then replied something to the effect of "well I guess we won't be doing business together then".

CLICK...

I was at first going to simply let it go and chalk it up to a failed attempt, however, during this time period I was reading Agrippa's three books of occult philosophy on the sacred texts website. In the foot notes there was commentary about a telepathy technique which is laid out as follows:

1. Write a letter to the person you wish to speak with

2. Place the letter in a sealed envelope

3. Burn the envelope while focusing on a link to the person

4. Focus and project the message until the envelope is fully burnt.

Now, to this recipe, I added a couple other elements, one being humor. I put a stamp on the envelope because you know... It will not go through without one.

I also wrote the address on the front as if it would be sent through the mail. Inside with the letter, I included a sigil which I made with 17hex's sigil generator (http://17hex.net/sigil/). The sigil was one of four that were made via the shoal technique of Gordon White mentioned here:

http://runesoup.com/2012/03/ultimate-sigil-magic-guide/.[2]

Before burning the envelope I cast a circle around a fire pit and did the LBRP (I don't think this was actually necessary, however, I did it because said ritual puts me in a focused meditative mood and I thought it would boost the effectiveness of the work).

I used a portion of the conversation we had on the phone as a mantra to focus on the target, keeping the sound of his voice in my mind's eye (or perhaps I should say my "minds ear"?). After the envelope was fully burnt, I clapped and laughed as a form of grounding/banishment to end the operation as suggested in Phil Hines Condensed Chaos. Then I went back to the office...

The following morning the prospect called me back saying he had a change of heart and would give me one chance to propose rates. He gave me the information I needed, and our program and cost blew the competitor's offerings out of the water. Within less than 4 months, I closed the deal.

Mission accomplished.

---

2. *http://runesoup.com/2012/03/ultimate-sigil-magic-guide/*

Closing:

For the open-minded magician, I hope that this book will serve as both a guide and a source of inspiration. I hope that you will either replicate the experiments within this tome, or use them as starting points for the development of your own magical operations in the context of sales and marketing adventures.

If you enjoyed this book, I would invite you to visit my website where you can preview and purchase other books of mine. https://jaboodaband.wixsite.com/nathandube

I would like to humbly thank you for reading this publication. I hope that it gives you a set of tools that will be useful on your own journey through kaocentric approaches to manifesting your desired life experiences.

Further reading and resources:

If you would like to further deepen your knowledge about magical technologies of which can be used to enhance your own practice, consider reading these books:

The Process of Magic by Taylor Ellwood

Financial Sorcery by Jason Miller

Pieces of Eight by Gordon White

The Seven Spheres by Rufus Opus

The Secret Keys of Conjure: Unlocking the Mysteries of American Folk Magic by Chas Bogan

The Encyclopedia of 5,000 Spells by Judika Illes

Psychic Witch by Matt Auryn

Weaving Fate by Aidan Wachter

Liber Null and Psychonaught by Peter Carol

Condensed Chaos by Phil Hine

Magical education courses for further study:

The Magical Experiments Courses by Taylor Ellwood

Rune Soup Premium Courses by Gordon White

Strategic Sorcery Course by Jason Miller

The Institute for Hermetic Studies Courses by Mark Stavish

About the Author

I am a musician, artist, digital marketing specialist, and author. Read more at jaboodaband.wixsite.com/nathandube.